Promises
for the
Golden Years

Harold Shaw Publishers
Wheaton, Illinois

Grateful acknowledgment is made to the publishers of the Scripture versions, portions of which are quoted in this book, using the following abbreviations:

KJV   *The King James Version*
NIV   *The New International Version*
NKJV   *The New King James Version*
Phillips *The New Testament In Modern English*
         by J. B. Phillips
RSV   *The Revised Standard Version*
TEV   *Today's English Version (Good News Bible)*
TLB   *The Living Bible*

The Holy Bible, New International Version, Copyright © 1978 by New York International Bible Society. Used by permission.
The Holy Bible, New King James Version, Copyright © 1979, 1980, 1982 by Thomas Nelson, Inc. Used by permission.
The New Testament in Modern English, revised edition by J. B. Phillips, Copyright © 1958, 1960, 1972, by J. B. Phillips. Used by permission of the Macmillan Publishing Company, Inc.
The Revised Standard Version of the Bible, Copyright 1946, 1952, © 1971, 1973. Used by permission.
Scripture quotations from TEV are from the *Good News Bible, The Bible in Today's English Version.* Copyright © 1976 by the American Bible Society. Used by permission.
The Living Bible, Copyright © 1971 by Tyndale House Publishers, Wheaton, Illinois. Used by permission.

Promises for the Golden Years is compiled and edited by Ann K. Alexander and Jean Hooten.

ISBN 0-87788-320-3
Printed in the United States of America
First printing, April 1983

How To Use Your Promise Book: The Three-Way System

"This God—his way is perfect; the promise of the Lord proves true." (Psalm 18:30)

God's Word, the Bible, is full of promises—promises made to his children whom he loves. Because God is God, and his very nature is truth, he cannot be unfaithful to these promises or his purposes. We can trust him to carry out completely all of his guarantees.

Promises for the Golden Years is a special selection of God's guarantees for those of you who have reached retirement age and beyond, whether you have served him all of your life or have just realized your need of him. Using the three steps described here you can find the promises and purposes that meet your specific needs.

As you use this book, remember that God made these promises

and he will keep them. Through prayer and practice they can become part of your life, giving you help, hope, and joy.

Step One:
Ask yourself, "What are my feelings right now? What are my struggles and fears? In what area of my life do I need to hear God's Word?" Look at the six sections of the index which starts on page 10— Who God Is, My Relationship to God, My Feelings, My Physical Condition, My Family, My Friends. Now turn to the section that *asks your question,* that fits your present situation. Read the verses slowly, letting God's Word fill your heart and mind.

Step Two:
Choose one of the verses which speaks especially to you. Below the verse write the date and one or two words that describe your present need. As you read the verse, claim it as God's promise to you. Know that he has given it to you! You may want to copy the verse

on a notecard and keep it with you to refer to, or maybe even memorize. (For fuller understanding, look it up in your Bible and read it in its context.)

Step Three:
Pray a short prayer to God thanking him for his promise to you (state it specifically as it applies to your situation). You may also wish to write it down in a notebook or on a prayer page at the end of this book. Return often to review the verses you have claimed and thank God for the ways you see him keeping his promises.

Applying the Three-Way System
Here are some illustrations of how *Promises for the Golden Years* may be used.

Illustration 1
Perhaps you have recently lost a loved one or you find that you must move hundreds of miles away from the place you have always called home. It seems that nothing is stable in your life anymore. God's promise to you might be one found on page 28 of this book:

Before you created the hills or brought the world into being, you were eternally God, and will be God forever. *Psalm 90:2 (TEV)*

You could write "too many changes" in your promise book and pray, "Dear Father, I am so tired of all these changes. I am losing everything that is familiar—my home, my friends, even the grocery store where I can find everything. But your Word says that you will always be God, and I claim that promise. Help me to hold tightly to your stability in the midst of all these changes and give me your peace. Thank you for who you are. In Jesus' name. Amen."

Illustration 2

Or, you may have ignored God all of your life and you wonder if he will listen to you now. This verse on page 24 may be the promise for you:

God so loved the world that he gave his only Son, that whoever believes in him should not perish but have eternal life. For God sent the Son into the world, not to condemn the world, but that the world might be saved through him. *John 3:16–17 (RSV)*.

You may write "Can God love me?" in your book and pray, "Dear God, I can hardly believe that you will give me everlasting life after the way I have ignored you. But now I understand that you give this gift to *whoever* believes regardless of past sins. I believe in you and I thank you for Christ's death for me. I claim this wonderful promise of new life. Thank you in your Son's holy name. Amen."

Finally

Remember, these are *God's* promises. If they are true now, they will prove true tomorrow and he will continue to carry them out again and again for the rest of your life!

Your Index to God's Promises & Purposes

Who God Is

• I have never given much thought to God. Can I turn to him now, when life seems to be closing in on me? *24*

• I have lived carelessly most of my life. Are my sins too many or too awful for God to forgive? *25*

• Some of the things I read and hear present opposing views of God. How can I know who he really is? *26*

• Everything around me is changing. Will God stay the same? *27*

My Relationship to God

• My faith is so shaky and I have so many doubts. Does God turn away from me when I am uncertain about him? *29*

• I have confessed my failures to God, but they keep haunting me. How can I be sure of God's forgiveness? *30*

• How can I show God my love and respect? *31*

• I am retired and all my days drag.

My Feelings

• As my body grows weaker and my senses fail, I am beginning to feel confused and lost. Can I depend on God for guidance and safety? *43*

• I am afraid to die. How can I overcome my fear of the unknown? *44*

• Will God be near me at the time of death? *45*

• What is heaven like? *46*

• My life is so empty. How can I find joy? *47*

• How can I overcome depression? *48*

• I am so anxious about all the unknown, uncertain things in my life. How can I find peace? *50*

• Loneliness seems to be more and more a part of my life. How can I turn this into something good rather than letting it defeat me? *51*

• If God has promised to be with me, why am I lonely? *52*

• The friends and family who used to fill my life have left me and I am alone. Will God abandon me too? *53*

My Physical Condition

• As my body and mind grow weaker, how can my faith grow stronger? *62*

• I long to be of help and service to those I love, but I am limited by fatigue and sickness. How can I help them? *63*

• I am concerned about being an embarrassment to my family because of actions I cannot control. *64*

• When I can no longer control my actions and speech, might I bring dishonor to the Lord? *66*

• I am concerned that others may soon be making decisions for me over which I have no control and with which I do not agree. *67*

• When I am no longer articulate and my mind is confused, will I still be able to communicate with God? *68*

• I am so afraid of sickness and pain. Will God give me the strength to endure? *69*

• Age has taken its toll on my appearance. Does this matter to God? *70*

• What can I look forward to in this life? *71*

My Family

• Sickness and age have pitifully changed someone dear to me and this makes me doubt God's goodness. How can I find assurance that he is a caring God? *73*

• Aging has altered the personality of my loved one. How can I accept this changed relationship with someone I love? *74*

• Who will take care of my loved ones when I am gone? *75*

• I am worried about money and about being an added burden to my children and their families. How does God want me to respond to my dependent condition? *76*

• My family ignores me, and doesn't seem to care what happens to me. How can I make them pay attention to me without resorting to whining and complaining? *77*

• I have sacrificed much for my family. Now they have everything and I have nothing, and I feel resentful. Can God change this resentment to appreciation and make me thankful for what I have? *78*

• I have been a good parent and have tried to bring my children up to lead a godly life. Some of them are not living for God. What hope can I have for them? *80*

• I haven't been a good parent, and my children are failures. I have received God's forgiveness, but is it too late for God to help my children? *81*

• I feel pain and guilt over my divorce. Does my failure mean God rejects me? *82*

My Friends

• Someone has done an injustice to a dear friend. I cannot forgive that person. How can I find victory and peace? *84*

• No one needs me. I have no one

to care for. How can an old person contribute to others?   *85*

• I feel that I have been over-looked and rejected. How can I overcome my bitterness?   *86*

• In my relationships I have built barriers instead of bridges. Is there any way I can overcome this and reach out to others?   *87*

• I know I have hurt a friend. What can I do to heal the harm I have done?   *88*

• Many of my dearest friends have died. Where can I find comfort? *90*

Who God Is

God seems threatening to me. He is so awesome and I feel so insignificant. Can I know him as a close, loving Father?

1. Ye shall seek me, and find me, when ye shall search for me with all your heart. And I will be found of you, saith the Lord. *Jeremiah 29:13–14 (KJV)*

☐_____

2. To all who received him, who believed in his name, he gave power to become children of God. *John 1:12 (RSV)*

☐_____

3. Even to your old age and gray hairs I am he, I am he who will sustain you. I have made you and I will carry you; I will sustain you and I will rescue you. *Isaiah 46:4 (NIV)*

☐_____

4. He is like a father to us, tender and sympathetic to those who reverence him. *Psalm 103:13 (TLB)*

☐_____

5. His Holy Spirit speaks to us deep in our hearts, and tells us that we really are God's children. *Romans 8:16 (TLB)*

☐_____

Selfishness, suffering, and evil abound in this world. Is there a caring God in the midst of all this?

1. This is how God showed his love among us: He sent his one and only Son into the world that we might live through him. *1 John 4:9 (NIV)*

☐_____

2. You will listen, O Lord, to the prayers of the lowly; you will give them courage. You will hear the cries of the oppressed and the orphans; you will judge in their favor, so that mortal men may cause terror no more. *Psalm 10:17–18 (TEV)*

☐_____

3. This plan of mine is not what

you would work out, neither are my thoughts the same as yours! For just as the heavens are higher than the earth, so are my ways higher than yours, and my thoughts than yours. *Isaiah 55:8–9 (TLB)*

☐_____

4. Know therefore that the Lord your God is God; he is the faithful God, keeping his covenant of love to a thousand generations of those who love him and keep his commands. *Deuteronomy 7:9 (NIV)*

☐_____

God seems so far away. Is he really active today? Does he make a difference in the world?

1. The Lord your God is he that goeth with you, to fight for you against your enemies, to save you. *Deuteronomy 20:4 (KJV)*

☐_____

2. We know that all things work together for good to them that love God, to them who are the called according to his purpose. *Romans 8:28 (KJV)*

☐————————————

3. Jesus Christ the same yesterday, and to day, and for ever. *Hebrews 13:8 (KJV)*

☐————————————

I can't feel or see God when I pray. Is he really listening? Will he help me?

1. The righteous cry, and the Lord heareth, and delivereth them out of all their troubles. *Psalm 34:17 (KJV)*

☐————————————

2. You will call upon me and come and pray to me, and I will listen to you. You will seek me and find me when you seek me with all your heart. *Jeremiah 29:12–13 (NIV)*

☐————————————

3. I am the Lord, who exercises kindness, justice and righteousness on earth, for in these I delight. *Jeremiah 9:24 (NIV)*

☐————————————

4. This is the confidence that we have in him, that, if we ask any thing according to his will, he heareth us: And if we know that he hear us, whatsoever we ask, we know that we have the petitions that we desired of him. *1 John 5:14–15 (KJV)*

☐_____

Many things happen over which I have no control. Does God really have control?

1. The Lord is still in his holy temple; he still rules from heaven. He closely watches everything that happens here on earth. *Psalm 11:4 (TLB)*

☐_____

2. God shall bring every work into judgment, with every secret thing, whether it be good, or whether it be evil. *Ecclesiastes 12:14 (KJV)*

☐_____

3. Ah Lord God! behold, thou hast made the heaven and the earth by thy great power and stretched out arm, and there is nothing too hard for thee . . . Behold, I am the Lord, the God of all flesh: is there any thing too hard for me? *Jeremiah 32:17, 27 (KJV)*

☐ _____

4. Yours, O Lord, is the greatness and the power and the glory and the majesty and the splendor, for everything in heaven and earth is yours. Yours, O Lord, is the kingdom; you are exalted as head over all. Wealth and honor come from you; you are the ruler of all things. In your hands are strength and power to exalt and give strength to all. *1 Chronicles 29:11–12 (NIV)*

☐ _____

Even my big problems are probably very small to the Creator of the universe. Does God really care about the details of my life?

1. I am poor and needy; yet the Lord thinketh upon me: thou art my help and my deliverer. *Psalm 40:17 (KJV)*

☐_____

2. Let him have all your worries and cares, for he is always thinking about you and watching everything that concerns you. *1 Peter 5:7 (TLB)*

☐_____

3. Fear not: for I have redeemed thee, I have called thee by thy name; thou art mine. *Isaiah 43:1 (KJV)*

☐_____

4. My God shall supply all your need according to his riches in glory by Christ Jesus. *Philippians 4:19 (KJV)*

☐_____

I'm not sure I can really rely on God. Will he keep his promises to me?

1. Let us hold on firmly to the hope we profess, because we can trust God to keep his promise. *Hebrews*

10:23 (TEV)

☐ _____

2. No matter how many promises God has made, they are "Yes" in Christ. *2 Corinthians 1:20 (NIV)*

☐ _____

3. The God who made both earth and heaven, the seas and everything in them. He is the God who keeps every promise. *Psalm 146:6 (TLB)*

☐ _____

I have never given much thought to God. Can I turn to him now, when life seems to be closing in on me?

1. God so loved the world that he gave his only Son, that whoever believes in him should not perish but have eternal life. For God sent the Son into the world, not to condemn the world, but that the world might be saved through him. *John 3:16–17 (RSV)*

☐ _____

2. He is patient with you, not wanting anyone to perish, but everyone to come to repentance. *2 Peter 3:9 (NIV)*

☐ _____

3. Repent, then, and turn to God, so that your sins may be wiped out, that times of refreshing may come from the Lord. *Acts 3:19 (NIV)*

☐ _____

4. This is what love is: it is not that we have loved God, but that he loved us and sent his Son to be the means by which our sins are forgiven. *1 John 4:10 (TEV)*

☐ _____

I have lived carelessly most of my life. Are my sins too many or too awful for God to forgive?

1. Listen! In this man Jesus, there is forgiveness for your sins! Everyone who trusts in him is freed from all guilt and declared righteous. *Acts 13:38–39 (TLB)*

☐ _____

2. You are a forgiving God, gracious and compassionate, slow to anger and abounding in love. *Nehemiah 9:17 (NIV)*

☐ _____

3. Let the wicked forsake his way, and the unrighteous man his thoughts: and let him return unto the Lord, and he will have mercy upon him; and to our God, for he will abundantly pardon. *Isaiah 55:7 (KJV)*

☐ _____

4. If we confess our sins, he is faithful and just to forgive us our sins, and to cleanse us from all unrighteousness. *1 John 1:9 (KJV)*

☐ _____

Some of the things I read and hear present opposing views of God. How can I know who he really is?

1. If ye continue in my word, then are ye my disciples indeed; and ye shall know the truth, and the truth shall make you free. *John 8:31–32 (KJV)*

□_____

2. I will bring the blind by a way that they knew not; I will lead them in paths that they have not known: I will make darkness light before them, and crooked things straight. These things will I do unto them, and not forsake them. *Isaiah 42:16 (KJV)*

□_____

3. The entrance of your words gives light. *Psalm 119:130 (NIV)*

□_____

4. Thou shalt guide me with thy counsel, and afterward receive me to glory. *Psalm 73:24 (KJV)*

□_____

Everything around me is changing. Will God stay the same?

1. I am the Lord, I change not. *Malachi 3:6 (KJV)*

□_____

2. Jesus Christ the same yesterday, and to day, and for ever. *Hebrews 13:8 (KJV)*

☐_____

3. Before you created the hills or brought the world into being, you were eternally God, and will be God forever. *Psalm 90:2 (TEV)*

☐_____

4. Every good and perfect gift is from above, coming down from the Father of the heavenly lights, who does not change like shifting shadows. *James 1:17 (NIV)*

☐_____

My Relationship to God

My faith is so shaky and I have so many doubts. Does God turn away from me when I am uncertain about him?

1. Even when we are too weak to have any faith left, he remains faithful to us and will help us, for he cannot disown us who are part of himself, and he will always carry out his promises to us. *2 Timothy 2:13 (TLB)*

☐ _____

2. By grace are ye saved through faith; and that not of yourselves: it is the gift of God. *Ephesians 2:8 (KJV)*

☐ _____

3. As a father has compassion on his children, so the Lord has compassion on those who fear him; for he knows how we are formed, he remembers that we are dust. *Psalm 103:13–14 (NIV)*

☐ _____

4. I am persuaded, that neither

death, nor life, nor angels, nor principalities, nor powers, nor things present, nor things to come, nor height, nor depth, nor any other creature, shall be able to separate us from the love of God, which is in Christ Jesus our Lord. *Romans 8:38–39 (KJV)*

☐ _____

I have confessed my failures to God, but they keep haunting me. How can I be sure of God's forgiveness?

1. I have blotted out, as a thick cloud, thy transgressions, and, as a cloud, thy sins: return unto me; for I have redeemed thee. *Isaiah 44:22 (KJV)*

☐ _____

2. O Lord, you are so good and kind, so ready to forgive; so full of mercy for all who ask your aid. *Psalm 86:5 (TLB)*

☐ _____

3. If we confess our sins, he is faith-

ful and just to forgive us our sins,
and to cleanse us from all unrighteousness. *1 John 1:9 (KJV)*

☐_____

4. Let the wicked forsake his way,
and the unrighteous man his
thoughts: and let him return unto
the Lord, and he will have mercy
upon him; and to our God, for he
will abundantly pardon. *Isaiah 55:7
(KJV)*

☐_____

How can I show God my love and respect?

1. What doth the Lord thy God
require of thee, but to fear the Lord
thy God, to walk in all his ways,
and to love him, and to serve the
Lord thy God with all thy heart
and with all thy soul. *Deuteronomy 10:12 (KJV)*

☐_____

2. If you love me, keep my commandments. *John 14:15 (NKJV)*

☐_____

3. So then, my brothers, because of God's great mercy to us, I make this appeal to you: Offer yourselves as a living sacrifice to God, dedicated to his service and pleasing to him. This is the true worship that you should offer. *Romans 12:1 (TEV)*

☐_____

4. He hath shewed thee, O man, what is good; and what doth the Lord require of thee, but to do justly, and to love mercy, and to walk humbly with thy God? *Micah 6:8 (KJV)*

☐_____

I am retired and all my days drag. Does God have any meaningful plans for my life?

1. I know the plans I have for you, says the Lord, plans for welfare and not for evil, to give you a future and a hope. *Jeremiah 29:11 (RSV)*

☐_____

2. You did not choose Me, but I chose you, and appointed you, that you should go and bear fruit, and that your fruit should remain: that whatever you ask the Father in My name, He may give you. *John 15:16 (NKJV)*

☐_____

3. You chart the path ahead of me, and tell me where to stop and rest. Every moment, you know where I am. You both precede and follow me, and place your hand of blessing on my head. *Psalm 139:3, 5 (TLB)*

☐_____

4. Warn them that are unruly, comfort the feebleminded, support the weak, be patient toward all men. See that none render evil for evil unto any man; but ever follow that which is good, both among yourselves, and to all men. Rejoice evermore. Pray without ceasing. In every thing give thanks: for this is the will of God in Christ Jesus concerning you. *1 Thessalonians 5:14–18 (KJV)*

☐_____

Most of my life is behind me. What kind of goals does God want me to make for the years I have left?

1. One thing I do, forgetting what lies behind and straining forward to what lies ahead, I press on toward the goal for the prize of the upward call of God in Christ Jesus. *Philippians 3:13–14 (RSV)*

☐ _____

2. Do your best to present yourself to God as one approved, a workman who does not need to be ashamed and who correctly handles the word of truth. *2 Timothy 2:15 (NIV)*

☐ _____

3. As you have therefore received Christ Jesus the Lord, so walk in him: rooted and built up in him, and established in the faith, as you have been taught, abounding in it with thanksgiving. *Colossians 2:6–7 (NKJV)*

☐ _____

4. We can be mirrors that brightly reflect the glory of the Lord. And as the Spirit of the Lord works within us, we become more and more like him. *2 Corinthians 3:18 (TLB)*

☐ _____

How can I develop a deep and lasting faith—one that doesn't shift from day to day?

1. The Lord will make you go through hard times, but he himself will be there to teach you, and you will not have to search for him any more. If you wander off the road to the right or the left, you will hear his voice behind you saying, "Here is the road. Follow it." *Isaiah 30:20–21 (TEV)*

☐ _____

2. Seek the Lord and his strength, seek his face continually. *1 Chronicles 16:11 (KJV)*

☐ _____

3. The Comforter, which is the Holy Ghost, whom the Father will send in my name, he shall teach you all things, and bring all things to your remembrance, whatsoever I have said unto you. *John 14:26 (KJV)*

☐ _____

4. When all kinds of trials and temptations crowd into your lives, my brothers, don't resent them as intruders, but welcome them as friends! Realise that they come to test your faith and to produce in you the quality of endurance. *James 1:2–3 (Phillips)*

☐ _____

I have received so much from God. I feel a burden of debt. How can I repay him?

1. If ye love me, keep my commandments. *John 14:15 (KJV)*

☐ _____

2. This is how we know what love is: Jesus Christ laid down his life for us. And we ought to lay down our lives for our brothers. *1 John 3:16 (NIV)*

☐ _____

3. I beseech you therefore, brethren, by the mercies of God, that ye present your bodies a living sacrifice, holy, acceptable unto God, which is your reasonable service. *Romans 12:1 (KJV)*

☐ _____

4. Every day I will praise you and extol your name for ever and ever. *Psalm 145:2 (NIV)*

☐ _____

5. Thou shalt love the Lord thy God with all thy heart, and with all thy soul, and with all thy mind. This is the first and great commandment. *Matthew 22:37–38 (KJV)*

☐ _____

Am I of any value to God?

1. God created man in his own image, in the image of God created he him; male and female created he them. *Genesis 1:27 (KJV)*

☐ _____

2. What is man, that thou art mindful of him? or the son of man, that thou visitest him? Thou madest him a little lower than the angels; thou crownedst him with glory and honour, and didst set him over the works of thy hands. *Hebrews 2:6–7 (KJV)*

☐ _____

3. Are not two sparrows sold for a farthing? And one of them shall not fall on the ground without your Father. But the very hairs of your head are all numbered. *Matthew 10:29–30 (KJV)*

☐ _____

4. Now you are no longer strangers to God and foreigners to heaven, but you are members of God's very own family, citizens of God's country, and you belong in God's household with every other Christian. *Ephesians 2:19 (TLB)*

☐ _____

When I don't *feel* God's presence, does that mean he is not with me?

1. He hath said, "I will never leave

thee, nor forsake thee." *Hebrews 13:5 (KJV)*

☐ _____

2. Lo, I am with you alway, even unto the end of the world. *Matthew 28:20 (KJV)*

☐ _____

3. Then shalt thou call, and the Lord shall answer; thou shalt cry, and he shall say, Here I am. *Isaiah 58:9 (KJV)*

☐ _____

4. How precious it is, Lord, to realize that you are thinking about me constantly! I can't even count how many times a day your thoughts turn towards me. And when I waken in the morning, you are still thinking of me! *Psalm 139:17–18 (TLB)*

☐ _____

5. Who shall separate us from the love of Christ? shall tribulation, or distress, or persecution, or famine, or nakedness, or peril, or sword? For I am persuaded, that neither death, nor life, nor angels, nor principalities, nor powers, nor things present, nor things to come, nor height, nor depth, nor any other creature, shall be able to separate us from the love of God, which is in Christ Jesus our Lord. *Romans 8:35, 38–39 (KJV)*

☐ _____

I've often thought I should read the Bible. Can it really say anything to me?

1. All those words which were written long ago are meant to teach us today; so that we may be encouraged to endure and to go on hoping in our own time. *Romans 15:4 (Phillips)*

☐ _____

2. All Scripture is given by inspiration of God, and is profitable for doctrine, for reproof, for correction, for instruction in righteousness: That the man of God may be perfect, thoroughly furnished unto all good works. *2 Timothy 3:16–17 (KJV)*

☐ _____

3. Thy word is a lamp unto my feet, and a light unto my path. The entrance of thy words giveth light; it giveth understanding unto the simple. *Psalm 119:105, 130 (KJV)*

□ _____

4. Your words are what sustain me; they are food to my hungry soul. They bring joy to my sorrowing heart and delight me. *Jeremiah 15:16 (TLB)*

□ _____

How can I be sure God really loves me?

1. I have loved thee with an everlasting love: therefore with lovingkindness have I drawn thee. *Jeremiah 31:3 (KJV)*

□ _____

2. God demonstrates his own love for us in this: While we were still sinners, Christ died for us. *Romans 5:8 (NIV)*

□ _____

3. The Lord is merciful and loving, slow to become angry and full of constant love. *Psalm 103:8 (TEV)*

☐ _____

4. In this was manifested the love of God toward us, because that God sent his only begotten Son into the world, that we might live through him. Herein is love, not that we loved God, but that he loved us, and sent his Son to be the propitiation for our sins. *1 John 4:9–10 (KJV)*

☐ _____

5. You are precious to me and honored, and I love you. *Isaiah 43:4 (TLB)*

☐ _____

My Feelings

As my body grows weaker and my senses fail, I am beginning to feel confused and lost. Can I depend on God for guidance and safety?

1. The Lord, he it is that doth go before thee; he will be with thee, he will not fail thee, neither forsake thee: fear not, neither be dismayed. *Deuteronomy 31:8 (KJV)*

□ _____

2. God hath not given us the spirit of fear; but of power, and of love, and of a sound mind. *2 Timothy 1:7 (KJV)*

□ _____

3. He will never let me stumble, slip or fall. For he is always watching, never sleeping. Jehovah himself is caring for you! He is your defender. He protects you day and night. He keeps you from all evil, and preserves your life. He keeps his eye upon you as you come and go, and always guards you. *Psalm*

121:3-8 (TLB)

□ _____

4. My grace is sufficient for thee: for my strength is made perfect in weakness. *2 Corinthians 12:9 (KJV)*

□ _____

I am afraid to die. How can I overcome my fear of the unknown?

1. He too shared in their humanity so that by his death he might destroy him who holds the power of death—that is, the devil—and free those who all their lives were held in slavery by their fear of death. *Hebrews 2:14-15 (NIV)*

□ _____

2. God so loved the world, that he gave his only begotten Son, that whosoever believeth in him should not perish, but have everlasting life. *John 3:16 (KJV)*

□ _____

3. I sought the Lord, and he heard me, and delivered me from all my fears. *Psalm 34:4 (KJV)*

□ _____

4. He will swallow up death in victory; and the Lord God will wipe away tears from off all faces; and the rebuke of his people shall he take away from off all the earth: for the Lord hath spoken it. *Isaiah 25:8 (KJV)*

☐ _____

Will God be near me at the time of death?

1. Yea, though I walk through the valley of the shadow of death, I will fear no evil: for thou art with me; thy rod and thy staff they comfort me. *Psalm 23:4 (KJV)*

☐ _____

2. I am persuaded, that neither death, nor life, nor angels, nor principalities, nor powers, nor things present, nor things to come, nor height, nor depth, nor any other creature, shall be able to separate us from the love of God, which is in Christ Jesus our Lord. *Romans 8:38–39 (KJV)*

☐ _____

3. God will redeem my soul from the power of the grave: for he shall receive me. *Psalm 49:15 (KJV)*

☐ _____

4. He will never abandon his people. They will be kept safe forever. *Psalm 37:28 (TLB)*

☐ _____

What is heaven like?

1. In my Father's house are many mansions: if it were not so, I would have told you. I go to prepare a place for you. *John 14:2 (KJV)*

☐ _____

2. The city has no need of sun or moon to shine upon it, for the glory of God is its light, and its lamp is the Lamb. *Revelation 21:23 (RSV)*

☐ _____

3. To him that overcometh will I give to eat of the tree of life, which is in the midst of the paradise of God. *Revelation 2:7 (KJV)*

☐ _____

4. I saw a new heaven and a new earth . . . And I heard a great voice out of heaven saying, Behold, the tabernacle of God is with men, and he will dwell with them, and they shall be his people, and God himself shall be with them, and be their God. *Revelation 21:1, 3–4 (KJV)*

□ _____

My life is so empty. How can I find joy?

1. Behold, I bring you good tidings of great joy, which shall be to all people. For unto you is born this day in the city of David a Saviour, which is Christ the Lord. *Luke 2:10–11 (KJV)*

□ _____

2. I will rejoice in the Lord, I will joy in the God of my salvation. *Habakkuk 3:18 (KJV)*

□ _____

3. Thou dost show me the path of life; in thy presence there is fulness of joy, in thy right hand are pleasures for evermore. *Psalm 16:11 (RSV)*

☐ _____

4. I will greatly rejoice in the Lord, my soul shall be joyful in my God; for he hath clothed me with the garments of salvation, he hath covered me with the robe of righteousness, as a bridegroom decketh himself with ornaments, and as a bride adorneth herself with her jewels. *Isaiah 61:10 (KJV)*

☐ _____

How can I overcome depression?

1. Base your happiness on your hope in Christ. When trials come endure them patiently; steadfastly maintain the habit of prayer. *Romans 12:12 (Phillips)*

☐ _____

2. The Lord is close to the brokenhearted and saves those who are crushed in spirit. *Psalm 34:18 (NIV)*

☐ _____

3. O my soul, why be so gloomy and discouraged? Trust in God! I shall again praise him for his wondrous help; he will make me smile again, *for he is my God! Psalm 43:5 (TLB)*

☐ _____

4. Just as you received Christ Jesus the Lord, so go on living in him—in simple faith. Yes, be rooted in him and founded upon him, continually strengthened by the faith as you were taught it and your lives will overflow with joy and thankfulness. *Colossians 2:6–7 (Phillips)*

☐ _____

5. Our light affliction, which is but for a moment, worketh for us a far more exceeding and eternal weight of glory; while we look not at the things which are seen, but at the things which are not seen: for the things which are seen are temporal; but the things which are not seen are eternal. *2 Corinthians 4:17–18 (KJV)*

☐ _____

I am so anxious about all the unknown, uncertain things in my life. How can I find peace?

1. Have no anxiety about anything, but in everything by prayer and supplication with thanksgiving let your requests be made known to God. And the peace of God, which passes all understanding, will keep your hearts and your minds in Christ Jesus. *Philippians 4:6–7 (RSV)*

☐_____

2. Peace I leave with you, my peace I give unto you; not as the world giveth, give I unto you. Let not your heart be troubled, neither let it be afraid. *John 14:27 (KJV)*

☐_____

3. These things I have spoken unto you, that in me ye might have peace. In the world ye shall have tribulation: but be of good cheer; I have overcome the world. *John 16:33 (KJV)*

☐_____

Loneliness seems to be more and more a part of my life. How can I turn this into something good rather than letting it defeat me?

1. Singing and making melody in your heart to the Lord; Giving thanks always for all things unto God and the Father in the name of our Lord Jesus Christ. *Ephesians 5:19b–20 (KJV)*

☐ _____

2. Base your happiness on your hope in Christ. When trials come endure them patiently; steadfastly maintain the habit of prayer. *Romans 12:12 (Phillips)*

☐ _____

3. Let each of you look not only to his own interests, but also to the interests of others. *Philippians 2:4 (RSV)*

☐ _____

4. I will remember the works of the Lord: surely I will remember thy wonders of old. I will meditate also of all thy work, and talk of thy doings. *Psalm 77:11–12 (KJV)*

☐ _____

If God has promised to be with me, why am I lonely?

1. Seek the Lord while he may be found, call upon him while he is near: let the wicked forsake his way, and the unrighteous man his thoughts: let him return to the Lord, and he will have mercy on him; and to our God, for he will abundantly pardon. *Isaiah 55:6–7 (NKJV)*

☐_____

2. The Lord is just in all his ways, and kind in all his doings. The Lord is near to all who call upon him, to all who call upon him in truth. *Psalm 145:17–18 (RSV)*

☐_____

3. Who shall separate us from the love of Christ? shall tribulation, or distress, or persecution, or famine, or nakedness, or peril, or sword? Nay, in all these things we are more than conquerors through him that loved us. *Romans 8:35, 37 (KJV)*

☐_____

The friends and family who used to fill my life have left me and I am alone. Will God abandon me too?

1. He hath said, I will never leave thee, nor forsake thee. *Hebrews 13:5b (KJV)*

☐_____

2. The mountains shall depart, and the hills be removed; but my kindness shall not depart from thee, neither shall the covenant of my peace be removed, saith the Lord that hath mercy on thee. *Isaiah 54:10 (KJV)*

☐_____

3. The Lord loves the just and will not forsake his faithful ones. They will be protected forever. *Psalm 37:28 (NIV)*

☐_____

4. The Lord your God is a merciful God; he will not abandon or destroy you or forget the covenant with your forefathers, which he confirmed to them by oath. *Deuteronomy 4:31 (NIV)*

☐_____

Mourning and sadness seem to be a part of my life now. Has God forgotten me?

1. Most assuredly, I say to you, that you will weep and lament, but the world will rejoice; and you will be sorrowful, but your sorrow shall be turned into joy. *John 16:20 (NKJV)*

☐_____

2. He healeth the broken in heart, and bindeth up their wounds. *Psalm 147:3 (KJV)*

☐_____

3. God shall wipe away all tears from their eyes; and there shall be no more death, neither sorrow, nor crying, neither shall there be any more pain: for the former things are passed away . . . Behold, I make all things new. *Revelation 21:4–5 (KJV)*

☐_____

4. Know therefore that the Lord your God is God; he is the faithful God, keeping his covenant of love to a thousand generations of those who love him and keep his commands. *Deuteronomy 7:9 (NIV)*

☐ _____

Life seems to belong to the young, and I feel increasingly useless. What use does God have for me?

1. White hair is a crown of glory and is seen most among the godly. *Proverbs 16:31 (TLB)*

☐ _____

2. If any one is in Christ, he is a new creation; the old has passed away, behold, the new has come. *2 Corinthians 5:17 (RSV)*

☐ _____

3. We are his workmanship, created in Christ Jesus unto good works, which God hath before ordained that we should walk in them. *Ephesians 2:10 (KJV)*

☐ _____

4. The righteous . . . are planted in the house of the Lord, they flourish in the courts of our God. They still bring forth fruit in old age, they are ever full of sap and green. *Psalm 92:12–14 (RSV)*

☐ _____

My Physical Condition

Fear and insecurity have made me physically ill. Must I always live like this?

1. The Lord is my light and my salvation; whom shall I fear? the Lord is the strength of my life; of whom shall I be afraid? *Psalm 27:1 (KJV)*

☐ _____

2. Bless the Lord, O my soul, and forget not all his benefits, who forgives all your iniquity, who heals all your diseases, who redeems your life from the pit, who crowns you with steadfast love and mercy, who satisfies you with good as long as you live so that your youth is renewed like the eagle's. *Psalm 103:2–5 (RSV)*

☐ _____

3. When thou passest through the waters, I will be with thee; and through the rivers, they shall not overflow thee: when thou walkest through the fire, thou shalt not be burned; neither shall the flame kindle upon thee. For I am the Lord thy God, the Holy One of Israel, thy Saviour. *Isaiah 43:2–3 (KJV)*

□ _____

4. Just as you trusted Christ to save you, trust him, too, for each day's problems; live in vital union with him. *Colossians 2:6 (TLB)*

□ _____

I am not able to get out and do anything. Can sitting and praying really accomplish anything?

1. Whatsoever we ask, we receive of him, because we keep his commandments, and do those things that are pleasing in his sight. And this is his commandment, that we should believe on the name of his Son Jesus Christ, and love one another, as he gave us commandment. *1 John 3:22–23 (KJV)*

□ _____

2. Have no anxiety about anything, but in everything, by prayer and supplication with thanksgiving let your requests be made known to God. And the peace of God, which passes all understanding, will keep your hearts and minds in Christ Jesus. *Philippians 4:6–7 (RSV)*

☐ _____

3. This is the confidence which we have in him, that if we ask anything according to his will he hears us. And if we know that he hears us in whatever we ask, we know that we have obtained the requests made of him. *1 John 5:14–15 (RSV)*

☐ _____

How can I share with others my knowledge and experience as I become increasingly incapacitated?

1. The righteous will flourish like a palm tree, they will grow like a cedar of Lebanon; planted in the house of the Lord, they will flourish in the courts of our God. They will still bear fruit in old age, they will stay fresh and green, proclaiming, "The Lord is upright; he is my Rock, and there is no wickedness in him." *Psalm 92:12–15 (NIV)*

☐ _____

2. Sanctify the Lord God in your hearts: and be ready always to give an answer to every man that asketh you a reason of the hope that is in you with meekness and fear. *1 Peter 3:15 (KJV)*

☐ _____

3. You may live a life worthy of the Lord and may please him in every way: bearing fruit in every good work, growing in the knowledge of God, being strengthened with all power according to his glorious might so that you may have great endurance and patience, and joyfully giving thanks to the Father, who has qualified you to share in the inheritance of the saints in the kingdom of light. *Colossians 1:10–12 (NIV)*

☐ _____

I want to be more pleasant, but I know I am becoming more irritable. What can I do about my temperament?

1. Be ye kind one to another, tenderhearted, forgiving one another, even as God for Christ's sake hath forgiven you. *Ephesians 4:32 (KJV)*
□_____

2. A soft answer turneth away wrath: but grievous words stir up anger. *Proverbs 15:1 (KJV)*
□_____

3. Bless the Lord, O my soul: and all that is within me, bless his holy name. Bless the Lord, O my soul, and forget not all his benefits. *Psalm 103:1–2 (KJV)*
□_____

4. As you know him better, he will give you, through his great power, everything you need for living a truly good life: he even shares his own glory and his own goodness with us! *2 Peter 1:3 (TLB)*
□_____

Some nights it's so hard for me to sleep. Can God help me rest?

1. I lie down and sleep; I wake again, for the Lord sustains me. *Psalm 3:5 (RSV)*
☐_____

2. He giveth his beloved sleep. *Psalm 127:2b (KJV)*
☐_____

3. Come to me, all you who are weary and burdened, and I will give you rest. Take my yoke upon you and learn from me, for I am gentle and humble in heart, and you will find rest for your souls. For my yoke is easy and my burden is light. *Matthew 11:28–30 (NIV)*
☐_____

4. He who dwells in the shelter of the Most High will rest in the shadow of the Almighty. *Psalm 91:1 (NIV)*
☐_____

As my body and mind grow weaker, how can my faith grow stronger?

1. We do not lose heart. Though outwardly we are wasting away, yet inwardly we are being renewed day by day. For our light and momentary troubles are achieving for us an eternal glory that far outweighs them all. So we fix our eyes not on what is seen, but on what is unseen. For what is seen is temporary, but what is unseen is eternal. *2 Corinthians 4:16–18 (NIV)*

☐_____

2. As you have therefore received Christ Jesus the Lord, so walk in him: rooted and built up in him, and established in the faith, as you have been taught, abounding in it with thanksgiving. *Colossians 2:6–7 (NKJV)*

☐_____

3. Let us therefore come boldly unto the throne of grace, that we may obtain mercy, and find grace to help in time of need. *Hebrews 4:16 (KJV)*

☐_____

I long to be of help and service to those I love, but I am limited by fatigue and sickness. How can I help them?

1. Warn them that are unruly, comfort the feebleminded, support the weak, be patient toward all men. See that none render evil for evil unto any man; but ever follow that which is good, both among yourselves, and to all men. Rejoice evermore. Pray without ceasing. In every thing give thanks: for this is the will of God in Christ Jesus concerning you. *1 Thessalonians 5:14–18 (KJV)*

☐ _____

2. Then the King will say to those on his right hand, Come, you blessed of my Father, inherit the kingdom prepared for you from the foundation of the world: for I was hungry, and you gave me food: I was thirsty, and you gave me drink: I was a stranger, and you took me in: I was naked, and you clothed me: I was sick, and you visited me: I was in prison, and you came to me. Inasmuch as you

64

did it unto one of the least of these my brethren, you did it to me. *Matthew 25:34–36, 40 (NKJV)*

□ _____

3. Giving all diligence, add to your faith virtue; and to virtue knowledge; and to knowledge temperance; and to temperance patience; and to patience godliness; and to godliness brotherly kindness; and to brotherly kindness charity. For if these things be in you, and abound, they make you that ye shall neither be barren nor unfruitful in the knowledge of our Lord Jesus Christ. *2 Peter 1:5–8 (KJV)*

□ _____

I am concerned about being an embarrassment to my family because of actions I cannot control.

1. Fear not; for thou shalt not be ashamed: neither be thou confounded; for thou shalt not be put to shame . . . With everlasting kindness will I have mercy on thee, saith the Lord thy Redeemer. *Isaiah 54:4a, 8b (KJV)*

☐ _____

2. I will lift up mine eyes unto the hills, from whence cometh my help. My help cometh from the Lord, which made heaven and earth. He will not suffer thy foot to be moved: he that keepeth thee will not slumber. The Lord is thy keeper: the Lord is thy shade upon thy right hand. *Psalm 121:1–3, 5 (KJV)*

☐ _____

3. I the Lord thy God will hold thy right hand, saying unto thee, Fear not; I will help thee. *Isaiah 41:13 (KJV)*

☐ _____

4. I will bring the blind by a way that they knew not; I will lead them in paths that they have not known: I will make darkness light before them, and crooked things straight. These things will I do unto them, and not forsake them. *Isaiah 42:16 (KJV)*

☐ _____

When I can no longer control my actions and speech, might I bring dishonor to the Lord?

1. Even to your old age and gray hairs I am he, I am he who will sustain you. I have made you and I will carry you; I will sustain you and I will rescue you. *Isaiah 46:4 (NIV)*

☐ _____

2. The very God of peace sanctify you wholly: and I pray God your whole spirit and soul and body be preserved blameless unto the coming of our Lord Jesus Christ. Faithful is he that calleth you, who also will do it. *1 Thessalonians 5:23–24 (KJV)*

☐ _____

3. The Lord, He is the one who goes before you. He will be with you, He will not leave you nor forsake you; do not fear nor be dismayed. *Deuteronomy 31:8 (NKJV)*

☐ _____

4. Now unto him that is able to keep you from falling, and to present you faultless before the pres-

3. I am persuaded, that neither death, nor life, nor angels, nor principalities, nor powers, nor things present, nor things to come, nor height, nor depth, nor any other creature, shall be able to separate us from the love of God, which is in Christ Jesus our Lord. *Romans 8:38–39 (KJV)*

☐_____

4. I am continually with thee: thou hast holden me by my right hand. Thou shalt guide me with thy counsel, and afterward receive me to glory. *Psalm 73:23–24 (KJV)*

☐_____

I am so afraid of sickness and pain. Will God give me the strength to endure?

1. The Lord is my light and my salvation; whom shall I fear? The Lord is the strength of my life; of whom shall I be afraid? *Psalm 27:1 (KJV)*

☐_____

2. Cast your cares on the Lord and he will sustain you; he will never let the righteous fall. *Psalm 55:22 (NIV)*

☐ _____

3. My God shall supply all your need according to his riches in glory by Christ Jesus. *Philippians 4:19 (KJV)*

☐ _____

4. He giveth power to the faint and to them that have no might he increaseth strength. Even the youths shall faint and be weary, and the young men shall utterly fall: but they that wait upon the Lord shall renew their strength; they shall mount up with wings as eagles; they shall run, and not be weary; and they shall walk, and not faint. *Isaiah 40:29–31 (KJV)*

☐ _____

Age has taken its toll on my appearance. Does this matter to God?

1. You shall also be a crown of

glory in the hand of the Lord, and a royal diadem in the hand of your God. *Isaiah 62:3 (NKJV)*

☐ _____

2. The Lord seeth not as man seeth; for man looketh on the outward appearance, but the Lord looketh on the heart. *1 Samuel 16:7 (KJV)*

☐ _____

3. O worship the Lord in the beauty of holiness. *Psalm 96:9 (KJV)*

☐ _____

What can I look forward to in this life?

1. Thou dost show me the path of life; in thy presence there is fulness of joy, in thy right hand are pleasures forevermore. *Psalm 16:11 (RSV)*

☐ _____

2. You have everything when you have Christ, and you are filled with God through your union with Christ. *Colossians 2:10 (TLB)*

☐ _____

3. Delight yourselves in the Lord, yes, find your joy in him at all times ... Never forget the nearness of your Lord. *Philippians 4:4–5 (Phillips)*

☐ _____

4. He guides the humble in what is right and teaches them his way. Who, then, is the man that fears the Lord? He will instruct him in the way chosen for him. *Psalm 25:9, 12 (NIV)*

☐ _____

My Family

Sickness and age have pitifully changed someone dear to me and this makes me doubt God's goodness. How can I find assurance that he is a caring God?

1. He has not despised or disdained the suffering of the afflicted one; he has not hidden his face from him but has listened to his cry for help. *Psalm 22:24 (NIV)*

☐_____

2. The mountains may depart and the hills be removed, but my steadfast love shall not depart from you, and my covenant of peace shall not be removed, says the Lord, who has compassion on you. *Isaiah 54:10 (RSV)*

☐_____

3. The Lord longs to be gracious to you; he rises to show you compassion. For the Lord is a God of justice. Blessed are all who wait for him! *Isaiah 30:18 (NIV)*

☐_____

4. Blessed be the God and Father of our Lord Jesus Christ, the Father of mercies and God of all comfort, who comforts us in all our affliction, so that we may be able to comfort those who are in any affliction, with the comfort with which we ourselves are comforted by God. For as we share abundantly in Christ's sufferings, so through Christ we share abundantly in comfort too. *2 Corinthians 1:3–5 (RSV)*
□ _____

Aging has altered the personality of my loved one. How can I accept this changed relationship with someone I love?

1. Trust in the Lord with all thine heart; and lean not unto thine own understanding. *Proverbs 3:5 (KJV)*
□ _____

2. We know that all things work together for good to them that love God, to them who are the called according to his purpose. *Romans 8:28 (KJV)*

□_____

3. A friend loveth at all times, and a brother is born for adversity. *Proverbs 17:17 (KJV)*

□_____

4. This is how we know what love is: Jesus Christ laid down his life for us. And we ought to lay down our lives for our brothers. *1 John 3:16 (NIV)*

□_____

Who will take care of my loved ones when I am gone?

1. I have been young, and now I am old; yet I have not seen the righteous forsaken or his children begging bread. *Psalm 37:25 (RSV)*

□_____

2. The young lions do lack, and suffer hunger: but they that seek the Lord shall not want any good thing. *Psalm 34:10 (KJV)*

□_____

3. He who did not grudge his own Son but gave him up for us all— can we not trust such a God to give us, with him, everything else that we can need? *Romans 8:32 (Phillips)*

☐_____

4. Know therefore that the Lord your God is God; he is the faithful God, keeping his covenant of love to a thousand generations of those who love him and keep his commands. *Deuteronomy 7:9 (NIV)*

☐_____

I am worried about money and about being an added burden to my children and their families. How does God want me to respond to my dependent condition?

1. Cast all your anxieties on him, for he cares about you. *1 Peter 5:7 (RSV)*

☐_____

2. The Lord thy God hath blessed

thee in all the works of thy hand: he knoweth thy walking through this great wilderness ... the Lord thy God hath been with thee; thou hast lacked nothing. *Deuteronomy 2:7 (KJV)*

□_____

3. God will supply every need of yours according to his riches in glory in Christ Jesus. *Philippians 4:19 (RSV)*

□_____

4. I have been young, and now I am old; yet I have not seen the righteous forsaken or his children begging bread. *Psalm 37:25 (RSV)*

□_____

My family ignores me, and doesn't seem to care what happens to me. How can I make them pay attention to me without resorting to whining and complaining?

1. I will sing of thy steadfast love, O Lord, for ever; with my mouth

I will proclaim thy faithfulness to all generations. For thy steadfast love was established for ever, thy faithfulness is firm as the heavens. *Psalm 89:1–2 (RSV)*

☐_____

2. Let each of you look not only to his own interests, but also to the interests of others. *Philippians 2:4 (RSV)*

☐_____

3. Love must be sincere. Hate what is evil; cling to what is good. Be devoted to one another in brotherly love. Honor one another above yourselves. Be joyful in hope, patient in affliction, faithful in prayer. *Romans 12:9–10, 12 (NIV)*

☐_____

4. A relaxed attitude lengthens a man's life; jealousy rots it away. *Proverbs 14:30 (TLB)*

☐_____

I have sacrificed much for my family. Now they have everything and I have nothing, and I feel resentful. Can God change this resentment to appreciation and make me thankful for what I have?

1. Be still before the Lord, and wait patiently for him; fret not yourself over him who prospers in his way ... Refrain from anger, and forsake wrath! Fret not yourself; it tends only to evil. *Psalm 37:7–8 (RSV)*

☐_____

2. Bless the Lord, O my soul, and forget not all his benefits: who forgiveth all thine iniquities; who healeth all thy diseases; who redeemeth thy life from destruction; who crowneth thee with lovingkindness and tender mercies; who satisfieth thy mouth with good things; so that thy youth is renewed like the eagle's. *Psalm 103:2–5 (KJV)*

☐_____

3. Let all bitterness, and wrath, and anger, and clamour, and evil speaking, be put away from you, with all malice: And be ye kind one to another, tenderhearted, forgiving one another, even as God for Christ's sake hath forgiven you. *Ephesians 4:31–32 (KJV)*

□_____

4. O my soul, don't be discouraged. Don't be upset. Expect God to act! For I know that I shall again have plenty of reason to praise him for all that he will do. He is my help! He is my God! *Psalm 42:11 (TLB)*

□_____

I have been a good parent and have tried to bring my children up to lead a godly life. Some of them are not living for God. What hope can I have for them?

1. He is patient with you, not wanting anyone to perish, but everyone to come to repentance. *2 Peter 3:9 (NIV)*

□_____

2. Have no anxiety about anything, but in everything by prayer and supplication with thanksgiving let your requests be made known to God. And the peace of

God, which passes all understanding, will keep your hearts and your minds in Christ Jesus. *Philippians 4:6–7 (RSV)*

□ _____

3. It is of the Lord's mercies that we are not consumed, because his compassions fail not. They are new every morning: great is thy faithfulness. It is good that a man should both hope and quietly wait for the salvation of the Lord. *Lamentations 3:22–23, 26 (KJV)*

□ _____

I haven't been a good parent, and my children are failures. I have received God's forgiveness, but is it too late for God to help my children?

1. Glory be to God who by his mighty power at work within us is able to do far more than we would ever dare to ask or even dream of—infinitely beyond our highest prayers, desires, thoughts, or hopes. *Ephesians 3:20 (TLB)*

□ _____

2. With men this is impossible; but with God all things are possible. *Matthew 19:26b (KJV)*

☐ _____

3. If ye turn again unto the Lord, your brethren and your children shall find compassion before them that lead them captive, so that they shall come again into this land: for the Lord your God is gracious and merciful, and will not turn away his face from you, if ye return unto him. *2 Chronicles 30:9 (KJV)*

☐ _____

4. The Lord is nigh unto all them that call upon him, to all that call upon him in truth. He will fulfil the desire of them that fear him: he also will hear their cry, and will save them. *Psalm 145:18–19 (KJV)*

☐ _____

I feel pain and guilt over my divorce. Does my failure mean God rejects me?

1. Listen! In this man Jesus, there

is forgiveness for your sins! Everyone who trusts in him is freed from all guilt and declared righteous— something the Jewish law could never do. *Acts 13:38–39 (TLB)*

☐ _____

2. Be merciful unto me, O Lord: for I cry unto thee daily. Rejoice the soul of thy servant: for unto thee, O Lord, do I lift up my soul. For thou, Lord, art good, and ready to forgive; and plenteous in mercy unto all them that call upon thee. *Psalm 86:3–5 (KJV)*

☐ _____

3. They will be like a well-watered garden, and they will sorrow no more . . . I will turn their mourning into gladness; I will give them comfort and joy instead of sorrow. *Jeremiah 31:12–13 (NIV)*

☐ _____

4. I know the plans I have for you, says the Lord, plans for welfare and not for evil, to give you a future and a hope. *Jeremiah 29:11 (RSV)*

☐ _____

My Friends

Someone has done an injustice to a dear friend. I cannot forgive that person. How can I find victory and peace?

1. Do not return evil for evil or reviling for reviling; but on the contrary bless, for to this you have been called, that you may obtain a blessing. *1 Peter 3:9 (RSV)*

☐ _____

2. Stop your anger! Turn off your wrath. Don't fret and worry—it only leads to harm. For the wicked shall be destroyed, but those who trust the Lord shall be given every blessing. *Psalm 37:8–9 (TLB)*

☐ _____

3. Do not say, "I'll pay you back for this wrong!" Wait for the Lord, and he will deliver you. *Proverbs 20:22 (NIV)*

☐ _____

4. Be ye kind one to another, tenderhearted, forgiving one another, even as God for Christ's sake hath forgiven you. *Ephesians 4:32 (KJV)*

☐ _____

No one needs me. I have no one to care for. How can an old person contribute to others?

1. Warn them that are unruly, comfort the feebleminded, support the weak, be patient toward all men. See that none render evil for evil unto any man: but ever follow that which is good, both among yourselves, and to all men. Rejoice evermore. Pray without ceasing. In every thing give thanks: for this is the will of God in Christ Jesus concerning you. *1 Thessalonians 5:14–18 (KJV)*

☐ _____

2. This is my commandment, that ye love one another, as I have loved you. Greater love hath no man than this, that a man lay down his life for his friends. *John 15:12–13 (KJV)*

☐ _____

3. Whatsoever ye do in word or deed, do all in the name of the Lord Jesus, giving thanks to God and the Father by him. *Colossians 3:17 (KJV)*

□ _____

I feel that I have been overlooked and rejected. How can I overcome my bitterness?

1. I am come that they might have life, and that they might have it more abundantly. *John 10:10b (KJV)*

□ _____

2. Whatsoever things are true, whatsoever things are honest, whatsoever things are just, whatsoever things are pure, whatsoever things are lovely, whatsoever things are of good report; if there be any virtue, and if there be any praise, think on these things . . . And the God of peace shall be with you. *Philippians 4:8–9 (KJV)*

□ _____

3. God is able to make all grace

abound to you, so that in all things at all times, having all that you need, you will abound in every good work. *2 Corinthians 9:8 (NIV)*

□ _____

4. Trust in him at all times; ye people, pour out your heart before him: God is a refuge for us. *Psalm 62:8 (KJV)*

□ _____

In my relationships I have built barriers instead of bridges. Is there any way I can overcome this and reach out to others?

1. Let love be genuine; hate what is evil, hold fast to what is good; love one another with brotherly affection; outdo one another in showing honor. Rejoice with those who rejoice, weep with those who weep. Live in harmony with one another; do not be haughty. *Romans 12:9–10, 15–16 (KJV)*

□ _____

2. Live in harmony with one another; be sympathetic, love as brothers, be compassionate and humble. Do not repay evil with evil or insult with insult, but with blessing, because to this you were called so that you may inherit a blessing. *1 Peter 3:8–9 (NIV)*

☐ _____

3. This is how we know what love is: Christ gave his life for us. We too, then, ought to give our lives for our brothers! *1 John 3:16 (TEV)*

☐ _____

4. Put on then, as God's chosen ones, holy and beloved, compassion, kindness, lowliness, meekness, and patience, forbearing one another and, if one has a complaint against another, forgiving each other; as the Lord has forgiven you, so you also must forgive. *Colossians 3:12–13 (RSV)*

☐ _____

I know I have hurt a friend. What can I do to heal the harm I have done?

1. Above all, love each other deeply, because love covers over a multitude of sins. *1 Peter 4:8 (NIV)*

☐_____

2. My prayer for you is that you will overflow more and more with love for others, and at the same time keep on growing in spiritual knowledge and insight, for I want you always to see clearly the difference between right and wrong, and to be inwardly clean, no one being able to criticize you from now until our Lord returns. May you always be doing those good, kind things which show that you are a child of God, for this will bring much praise and glory to the Lord. *Philippians 1:9–11 (TLB)*

☐_____

3. All of you be subject one to another, and be clothed with humility: for God resisteth the proud, and giveth grace to the humble. Humble yourselves therefore under the mighty hand of God, that he may exalt you in due time. *1 Peter 5:5–6 (KJV)*

☐_____

Many of my dearest friends have died. Where can I find comfort?

1. I, even I, am he that comforteth you. *Isaiah 51:12 (KJV)*

☐ _____

2. He healeth the broken in heart, and bindeth up their wounds. *Psalm 147:3 (KJV)*

☐ _____

3. Yea, though I walk through the valley of the shadow of death, I will fear no evil: for thou art with me; thy rod and thy staff they comfort me. *Psalm 23:4 (KJV)*

☐ _____

4. Blessed be God, even the Father of our Lord Jesus Christ, the Father of mercies, and the God of all comfort; who comforteth us in all our tribulation, that we may be able to comfort them which are in any trouble, by the comfort wherewith we ourselves are comforted of God. *2 Corinthians 1:3–4 (KJV)*

☐ _____

Prayer Page

date   prayer

_____

_____

_____

date   prayer

_____

_____

_____

date   prayer

_____

_____

_____

date   **prayer**

_____

_____

_____

_____

_____

date   **prayer**

_____

_____

_____

_____

_____

date   **prayer**

_____

_____

_____

_____

_____

date   **prayer**

_____

_____

_____

_____

date   **prayer**

_____

_____

_____

_____

date   **prayer**

_____

_____

_____

_____

date   **prayer**

_____

_____

_____

_____

date   **prayer**

_____

_____

_____

_____

date   **prayer**

_____

_____

_____

_____